RUGBY SIMPLIFIED

RUGBY 101 FOR BEGINNER PARENTS

WRITTEN BY
CHARLIE PURDON & WARWICK AUSTIN

Book design: Jasmine Vowels.

TABLE OF CONTENTS

1. Rugby values
2. Parents code of conduct
3. Brief history
4. State of the game
5. Rugby World Cup
6. Playing positions
7. Field dimensions
8. Ball dimensions
9. Simplified rugby rules
10. Referee signals
11. Basic rugby glossary
12. Alternative terms and analogies
13. Banter 101

1. RUGBY VALUES

TEAMWORK - Learning to work with other people from a variety of different background collectively for a common goal is a lifelong skill. Building and maintaining relationships are essential in all aspects of life.

PASSION - Rugby brings out enthusiasm, emotion and a strong sense of compassion towards the belonging of something that is far greater than oneself.

DISCIPLINE - Building a good work ethic is important to success in anything. Setting goals, being driven and self motivated to achieve something is one of the most rewarding feelings in life. Discipline teaches you about consequences on and off the field. Through rugby, discipline ensures a player creates good lifelong habits.

RESILIENCE - Learning to be mentally tough through all sorts of adversity. Dealing with loss, never giving up and coming back from injuries are all massive in building one's character and contributing to the team's culture. Culture is to a team what personality is to an individual.

RESPECT - A core value to any individual is that of respect, for the game, its code of ethics, opposition, teammates coaches and yourself. Learning to have good manners and being polite will put the player in good stead for the future.

INTEGRITY - Iconic former British and Irish Lions coach, Jim Telfer once said, "There's two types of rugby players, there is honest one's then there is the rest." You can't hide from the man in the mirror. Learning to be authentic, accountable and responsible are all vital in setting standards on how you want to be perceived as a person and how much you want to achieve as a player and in life. The game has no sentiment. Rugby is the ultimate equalizer and it's important to always show humility as you're only as good as your next performance.

FRIENDSHIP - Rugby gives you the opportunity to make new friends all over the world. It forces you to get out your comfort zone and grow as an individual. Rugby provides a perfect platform for networking and creating connections with people that you could reach out to later in life.

SPORTSMANSHIP - Teaches you to play fair, ethically, behave well and treat others with empathy.

ENJOYMENT - Sports first and foremost is about fun!

2. PARENT'S CODE OF CONDUCT

SHOW RESPECT FOR ALL PLAYERS AND OFFICIALS

ALWAYS BE VERBALLY SUPPORTIVE IN A PROACTIVE MANNER

APPLAUD GOOD PLAY AND DEMONSTRATE POSITIVE SUPPORT FOR ALL PARTICIPANTS

RECOGNIZE THE IMPORTANCE OF VOLUNTEERS AND THANK THEM FOR THEIR EFFORTS

DO NOT STRAY ONTO THE FIELD OF PLAY AT ANY TIMES

DO NOT VERBALLY ABUSE MATCH OFFICIALS OR COACHES

DO NOT USE BAD LANGUAGE, CURSE OR ENCOURAGE PHYSICAL VIOLENCE

DO NOT BECOME INVOLVED IN AN ALTERCATION WITH FELLOW OR OPPOSITION PARENTS

3. BRIEF HISTORY

Never let the truth get in the way of a good story they say, and when it comes to the origins of rugby, we like to let 'legend' or 'myth' take preference to 'claim' or 'conspiracy.'

A long, long time ago, before gridiron, before baseball and before Facebook, there was a boy named William Webb Ellis. Aged 17, in the year 1823 at Rugby School in Warwickshire during a football (soccer) match, the rebellious and revolutionary Webb Ellis would change the face of sport, and the world, with one simple disobedience of the laws of the game.

When the football was kicked in the direction of young Will, he not only opted to catch and thus handle the ball, but he so too opted to carry the ball forward towards the opposition goals. His teammates and opposition alike stood in amazement, clearly knowing at the time that what their classmate had done was form the origins of a game that would nearly 200 years later gather a global following of 475 million fans.

Yes, it was a cheeky English schoolboy who is widely credited with starting the game played in heaven. With poetic commemoration at his old school lies a plaque in his honour which reads:

**THIS STONE
COMMEMORATES THE EXPLOIT OF
WILLIAM WEBB ELLIS
WHO WITH A FINE DISREGARD FOR THE RULES OF FOOTBALL
AS PLAYED IN HIS TIME
FIRST TOOK THE BALL IN HIS ARMS AND RAN WITH IT
THUS ORIGINATING THE DISTINCTIVE FEATURE OF
THE RUGBY GAME
AD 1823**

To this day, both the school and the boy are part and parcel of the game they so greatly influence. The school, quite naturally, in the name of the game, while The Webb Ellis Cup, affectionately known as Bill, is the trophy that is handed to the winner of the Rugby World Cup every four years.

IN THE SHADOW OF HISTORY: A SCHOOL PLAQUE MARKS WEBB ELLIS' RUN, CALLING HIS DECISION TO PICK UP THE BALL 'A FINE DISREGARD FOR THE RULES'

4. STATE OF THE GAME

World Rugby states that there are around 475 million rugby fans in the world - that's more than the entire US population.

It truly is a global sport with some 3.2 million player listed globally and a further 5.3 million non-registered players.

From Andorra to Zimbabwe, there are a total of 119 countries that play rugby. The biggest of which, in terms of players, is England with over 2 million players.

Outside of the World Cup, the other major tournaments are the Rugby Championship (Argentina, Australia, New Zealand and South Africa) and the Six Nations (England, Ireland, Italy, France, Scotland, and Wales). There are also several provincial and club competitions that take place in the various countries, with a few intercontinental championships. Most notably Super Rugby (featuring club teams from the Rugby Championship nations as well as Japan) and the European Rugby Champions Cup (featuring club teams from the Six Nations countries).

Despite their relatively small population of just less than 5 millions people, New Zealand is the dominant force in rugby. Other than being the number one ranked team in the world, they have the most World Cup titles (3), the most Rugby Championship titles (15) and they boast a winning percentage of close on 80% from nearly 600 Test matches.

Rugby reached new heights in 2016 with the re-introduction of sevens to the Olympics for the first time since 1924. The game continues to grow through both the men and women's game in the sevens arena with a wider variety of countries participating on the World Sevens Series circuit in comparison to the 15-a-side version.

5. RUGBY WORLD CUP

According to World Rugby, the Rugby World Cup is the third biggest sporting event behind the world behind the Olympics and the FIFA World Cup. That's a pretty big deal.

The first ever Rugby World Cup was played co-hosted by New Zealand and Australia in 1987 and has since been played in England, Ireland, Wales, France, and South Africa. Japan will host the next installment of the competition in 2019.

There were several attempts to set up a Rugby World Cup in the early 1980s, but it was a joint proposal by the Australian Rugby Union and the New Zealand Rugby Football Union presented to the International Rugby Football Union (now World Rugby) that got the tournament greenlit in 1985.

Initially, the tournament was played by invitation basis, and from 1991 onward it became qualification based.

It is played every four years and in its current format, comprises of 20 teams split across four pools, after which the top two teams in each pool progress to the Quarter-finals as the knockout stages commence.

New Zealand boasts the most titles, having lifted the Webb Ellis Cup on three occasions in 1987, 2011 and 2015. Australia (1991 and 1999) and South Africa (1995 and 2007) have two titles apiece, with England's 2003 win being the only by a Northern Hemisphere nation.

Some interesting facts:

25 - The number of teams to have played in Rugby World Cup tournaments since 1987.

145 - The number of points scored by New Zealand against Japan in 1995. The record for a single World Cup match.

277 - The number of points Jonny Wilkinson of England has scored in World Cups - the most in history.

15 - The record number of tries scored in World Cup history, jointly held by Jonah Lomu (New Zealand) and Bryan Habana (South Africa).

0 - Number of tries scored in the 2007 Final, which was won 15-6 by South Africa against England.

THE WILLIAM WEBB ELLIS TROPHY SITS ON THE SIDELINE DURING THE IRB 2011 RUGBY WORLD CUP POOL D MATCH BETWEEN FIJI AND NAMIBIA AT ROTORUA INTERNATIONAL STADIUM ON SEPTEMBER 10, 2011 IN ROTORUA, NEW ZEALAND.

6. PLAYING POSITIONS

FIFTEEN A SIDE RUGBY:
TIGHT FIVE

1 - LOOSEHEAD PROP

- Large, hairy, manly men. Inherently aggressive on the field yet nice and polite off it.
- Often the best beer guzzlers on the team and almost always the funniest.
- Primary roles include pushing in the front row of the scrum, lifting in the lineout, moving bodies at the ruck, and the odd ball carry if lucky enough to catch it.

2 - HOOKER

- Too short to play prop, too slow to play loose-forward, the hooker is the aggressive enforcer who runs around like a nutter frothing at the mouth, looking to get involved wherever possible.
- Often goes bald in later years
- Primary role is to throw the ball in the line-out, hook the ball in the scrum, attend rucks, and get through as many tackles as possible

3 - TIGHTHEAD PROP

- Much like that of the loosehead in terms of physical appearance and personality traits.
- Unlike the loosehead, the tighthead is packing their head down in the scrum between the opposition's hooker and loosehead.
- Other than usual prop rules, the tighthead is responsible for anchoring the right side of the scrum which gives the backline a good platform from which to attack on the preferable right side of the field.

4/5. LOCK

- Locks are generally the tallest players on the field and for the most part very goofy and inarticulate.

- Primary roles would include jumping in the line-out and pushing on the backsides of the props in the scrum.

- The useful ones are usually very effective at carrying the ball and clearing bodies off the ball at the ruck.

LOOSE-FORWARDS

6 - BLINDSIDE FLANK

- Flanks generally should be the fittest players on the field because of the sheer amount of running and tackling they're expected to do.

- They are expected to poach the ball off of the opposition at the breakdown and ultimately be a disruptive menace wherever possible.

- Blindside flank would always pack down at the scrum on the narrower side of the field, (blindside).

7 - OPENSIDE FLANK

- Similar behavior to that of blindside flank but always packs down at the scrum on the wider side of the field, (openside).

- Openside is usually first arriving player to the breakdown from a scrum.

8 - EIGHTHMAN

- No. 8 as they are often referred to, are generally the better looking of the loose-forwards.

- Multi-rolled player link between the forwards and backs on attack because of superior race-horse like athleticism. Often tall and used as a line-out jumper.

HALFBACKS / INSIDE BACKS

9 - SCRUM-HALF / HALFBACK

- They are generally a tiny chap with a big voice and a serious Napoleon complex, who barks orders without fear.

- He is the link between the forwards and the backs, where he feeds the ball into the scrum, distributing it from the forwards to the backs swiftly and with accuracy.

- His other roles would include organizing the defense line, game management and relieving pressure with the boot if needed.

10 - FLYHALF / FIRST FIVE-EIGHTH

- Usually has the dubious task of being the leader of the backline, 'the pretty boy.'

- Must have a cool and calm demeanor in order to deal with chaos around him and have the vision to exploit opposition defensively.

- Often slight of hand to have the ability to pass the ball accurately to his fellow backs.

- Most often the primary kicker to put his/her team in a good territory of the field.

CENTERS / MIDFIELDERS

12 - INSIDE CENTER/SECOND FIVE-EIGHTH

- Often a hard-hitter on defense or a hard-charger on the attack with lovely ball distribution skills to match.

- Generally expected to make a lot of front on tackles in the mid-field or poach/disrupt a lot of opposition ball at the breakdown.

- Mr. Dependable - stocky, tough, uncompromising.

13 - OUTSIDE CENTER

- Generally the more nimble and shifty of the two midfielders.

- Creates a lot of scoring opportunities in the wider channels of the field on attack.

- Expected to be a leader on defense and anticipate the opposition movement and shape.

BACK THREE / OUTSIDE BACKS

11 - LEFT WING

- Lines up on the left side of the field.

- Wing or winger is generally the quickest players of the team. They are expected to finish try scoring opportunities and claim a majority of the glamour and fame.

- Need to have excellent aerial skills as they get a lot of balls kicked on them or chasing a lot of kicks.

- Defensively must chase down linebreaks, complete one-on-one tackles and secure breakdowns in the wider channels.

14 - RIGHT WING

- Lines up on the right side of the field.

- Same as above.

15 - FULLBACK

- Mostly an observer from the back waiting for the right moment to pounce.

- Pivotal on the counter-attack and inserting themselves between the centers and wingers.

- Excellent aerial skills and a strong kicking game.

- Last line on defense - expected to make a lot of open field one-on-one tackles.

In 15's rugby, you are allowed to have 8 reserve players, usually 5 forwards and 3 backline players.

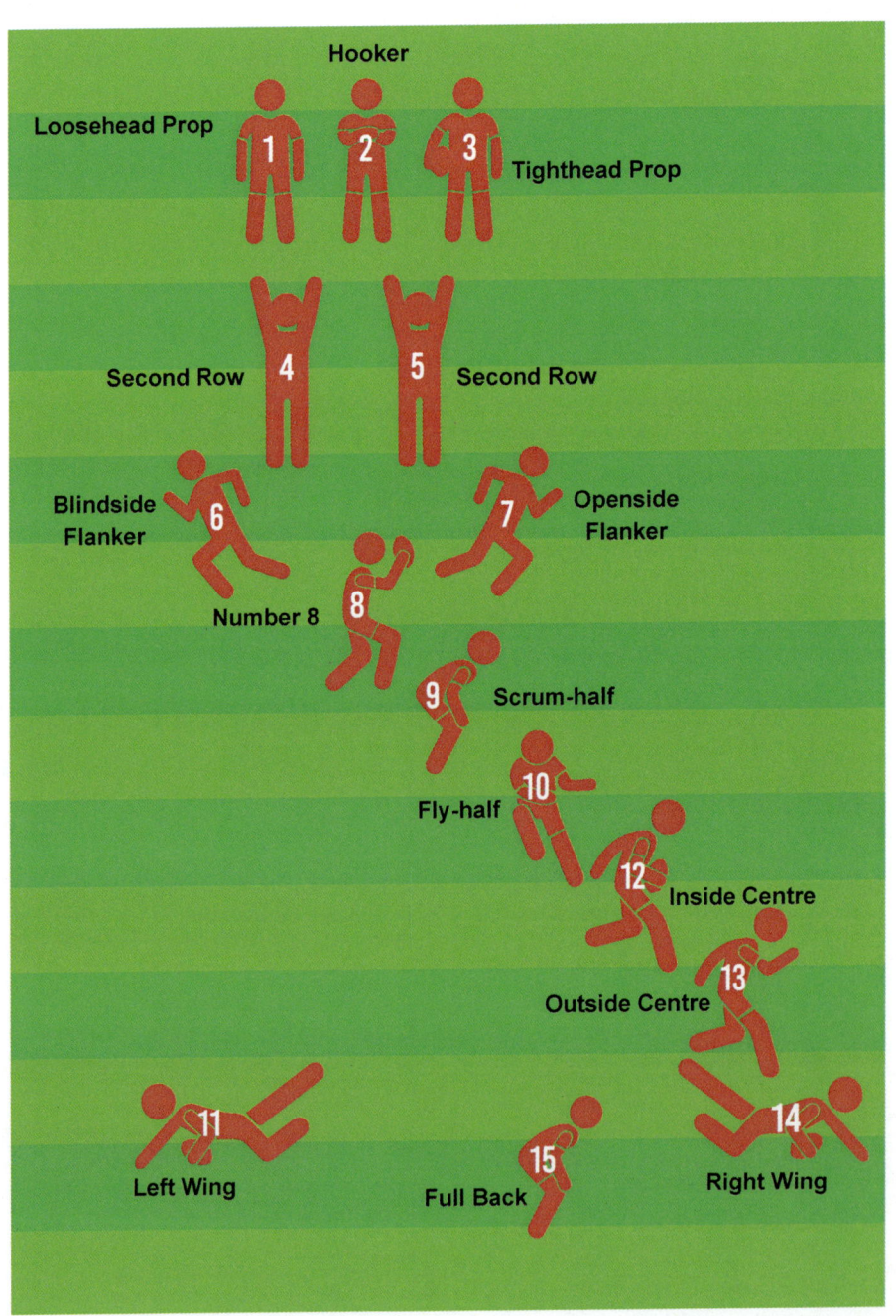

SEVEN A SIDE RUGBY:

FORWARDS

LOOSEHEAD PROP - Generally a taller player and very quick out of the scrum. Usually the primary line-out jumper.

HOOKER - Very strong and powerful. Good over the ball and highly skilled.

TIGHTHEAD - The strongest player on the team. They must be able to stabilize the right side of the scrum.

BACKS

SWEEPER - Very quick. A playmaker and good one-on-one defender.

1ST RECEIVER - Primary playmaker, highly skilled.

CENTRE - Good playmaker. Very quick and good defender.

WING - Lots of speed, good finisher and defender.

In 7's rugby, teams would have 5 reserves, preferably utility players who can play more than one position.

Rugby players are either piano shifters or piano movers. Fortunately, I am one of those who can play a tune.

— Pierre Danos

7. FIELD DIMENSIONS

These are regulation dimensions of a full sized rugby field, although many youth and junior age groups matches would be played on a smaller sized field.

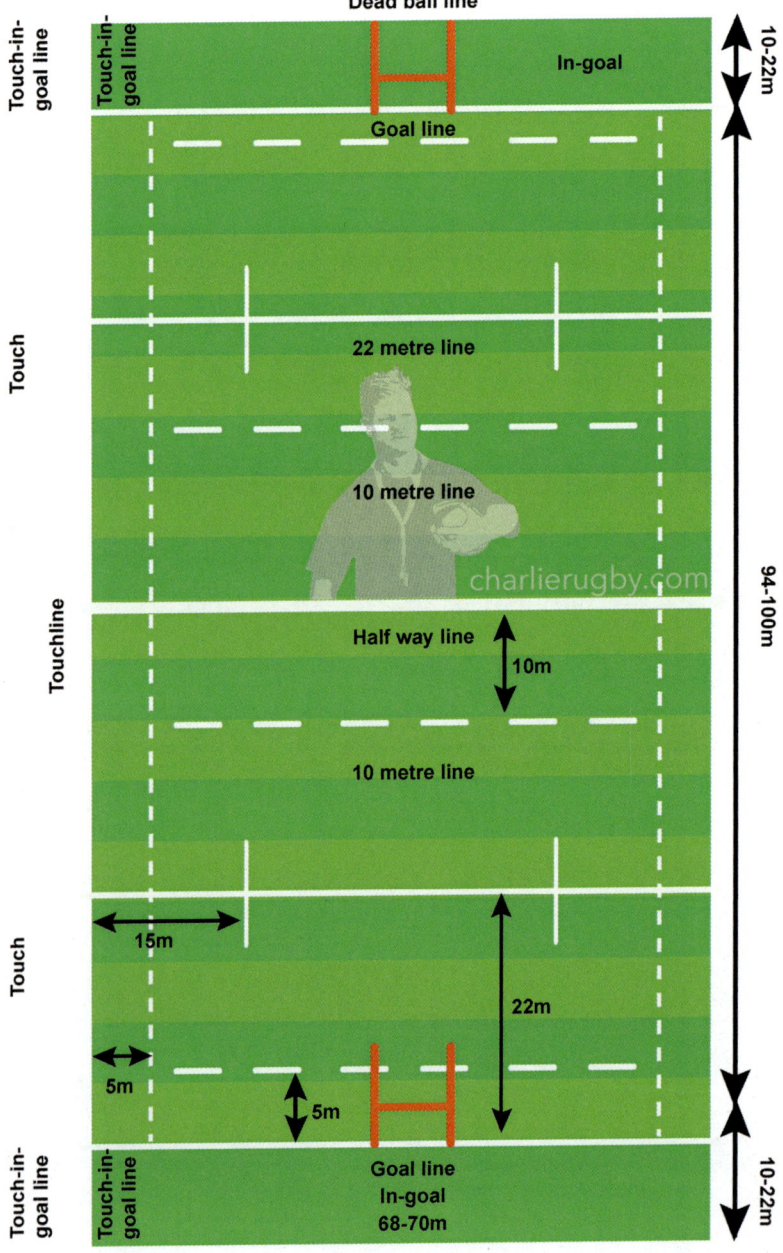

8. BALL DIMENSIONS

In most countries, players start off by using a size 3 ball which is a lot smaller and lighter in weight, generally from u7-u10. From u11-u14 players would use a size 4 ball then from u15 upwards they'd play with a regulation size 5 ball. The dimensions of this ball are indicated below.

Regular Size 5 ball dimensions.

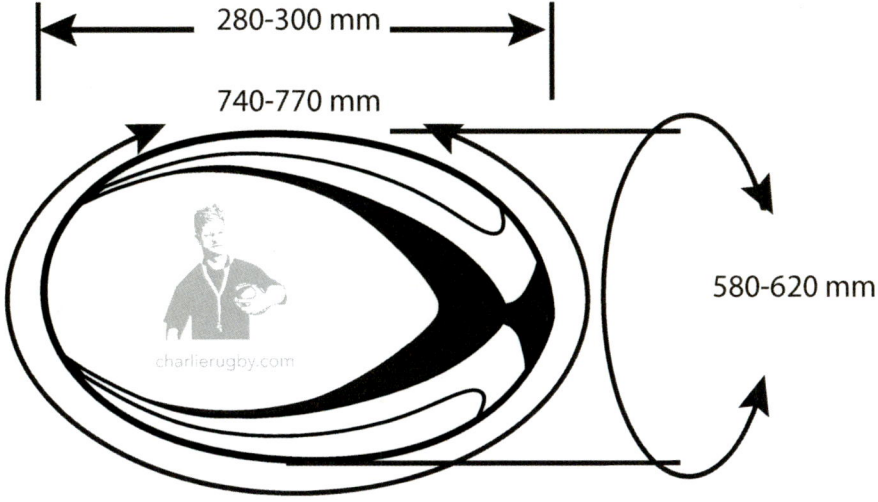

280-300 mm
740-770 mm
580-620 mm

In 1823, William Webb Ellis first picked up the ball in his arms and ran with it. And for the next 156 years forwards have been trying to work out why.
- Sir Tasker Watkins

9. SIMPLIFIED RUGBY RULES

Below is a fundamental, simplified explanation of general rugby rules. It does not include every single intricate detail but is more than sufficient for a beginner rugby parent.

NUMBER OF PLAYERS

- Each team must have no more than fifteen players on the field at all times.

- In 7's rugby - each team has no more than 7 players on the field at all times.

In a regular match day squad, there are 23 players per team. 15 starters and 8 reserves.

TIME

- A game of rugby has two periods of 40 minutes each with a 10min interval called half time.

- The majority of youth games are played for a much shorter period of time, often mutually agreed upon by both coaches.

- In the USA, the majority of u14 - u16 matches are played over two periods of 30 minutes with the u18 matches played over two periods of 35 minutes.

OFFICIALS

A Referee officiates every match in the center of the field, assisted by two judges or assistant referees who are stationed on the touch lines with a flag to indicate when the ball crosses the touchline.

METHODS OF SCORING

TRY - When a player in control of the ball grounds it in the opponents' in goal, a try is scored. A try is worth 5 points.

PENALTY TRY - If a player would likely have scored a try but is stopped by an act of foul play by an opponent, a penalty try is awarded. No conversion attempted. A penalty try is worth 7 points.

CONVERSION - Once a try is scored, it gives the scorers team an attempt to gain another 2 points by taking a kick at goal. The kick is made in line with where the ball was grounded. The conversion kick can be a drop kick or place kick. The kicker has 90 seconds from when the try is scored to make the kick. The opposition must line up behind the try line and are allowed to chase and charge down the kick after the kicker has begun his runup.

PENALTY GOAL - When a team chooses to kick the ball at goal to gain 3 points from a penalty. The opposition team must line up at a minimum 10m away and are not allowed to move, charge the kick or shout.

DROPPED GOAL - A player scores a drop goal by kicking a dropkick through the posts in general play. A dropped goal is worth 3 points.

In seven-a-side rugby, all conversions and penalty goal's are drop kicked and not place kicked.

KICK-OFF AND RESTART KICKS
The kick-off occurs at the start of each half of the match, and a restart occurs after a score by the opposition.

- The start of the game, the team whose captain wins the coin toss elects which team will kick off to start the game, after the interval the team who received the kick off at the start, kicks off the next half.

- The kicker must take the kick from the center of the halfway line.

- The kickoff and restart must travel past the opponents 10m line. If it doesn't, a scrum is awarded to the opposition in the center of the halfway line.

- The team kicking off must remain behind the ball when it is being kicked. If they do not, a midfield scrum will be rewarded to opposition team.

- If the kick goes directly into touch, the opposition can choose between allowing opposition to kickoff again or a scrum on center of halfway line.

- If the ball doesn't travel past 10m line and the opposition plays the ball then its play on.

It's important to note that in seven-a-side rugby, the restart kick-off is taken by the try scoring team.

22M DROP-OUT

A drop out is a drop kick taken by the defending team anywhere behind the 22m line and is a result of an attacking player kicking or running the ball over the dead ball line or when an attacking player retrieves the ball in the in goal area and grounds it. The ball may not be taken back into the in-goal area and ground by the defending player - that will result in a 5m scrum to the initial attacking team.

- The drop-out kick has to cross the 22m line.

- Team kicking must remain behind kicker while the ball is being kicked.

KNOCK-ON

A knock-on occurs when a player loses control of the ball and it travels in a forward direction, towards the opposing team's dead ball line. When a player knocks the ball forward - a scrum is awarded to the opposition.

FORWARD PASS
When a player throws or passes the ball to a teammate who is in front of the passing player.. When a forward pass occurs - a scrum is awarded to the opposition.

TACKLE
A tackle occurs when the ball carrier is held by one or more opponents and is brought to the ground.

- When the player has one knee on the ground, that player has been 'brought to ground'.

- The tackler must release the tackled player and get up or move away from tackled player.

- The tackled player must place the ball or release it immediately.

TACKLE LAWS

1. You may not tackle a player who is not in possession of the ball.

2. The tackler must attempt to wrap their arms around the ball carrier for a tackle to be legal.

3. The tackler CANNOT grasp the player above the line of the ball carriers shoulders.

4. The tackler CANNOT pick the ball carrier up off the ground, turn their body through 90 degrees and drive him into the ground.

5. The tackler may not trip a ball carrier with his feet.

RUCK

A ruck is formed when one or more players from each team, who are on their feet, in physical contact, close around the ball on the ground. Once the ruck is formed, a player is not allowed to use their hands to retrieve the ball, only their feet.

RUCK LAWS

1. Players in a ruck must endeavor to stay on their feet.

2. A player must not intentionally fall or kneel in a ruck.

3. A player must not jump on the ruck or intentionally collapse it.

4. Once the ball is out of the ruck, a player may not return the ball into the ruck.

5. Once the ruck is formed, a player is not allowed to use their hands to retrieve the ball, only their feet.

6. The tackler, prior to the formation of a ruck, may not fall or lay on the ball and must move or roll away from the ball immediately.

OFFSIDES AND ONSIDES

OFFSIDES AT THE RUCK
A player is offsides if he is in front of the hindmost foot of the player at the ruck. Players may only move forward once the ball has left the scrumhalf's hands.

OFFSIDES AT THE MAUL
A player is offsides after a line-out maul if he encroaches past the ten meter line, before the referee indicates that it is safe to do so. After which, the offsides line is the hindmost foot of the player at maul. Players may only enter the maul from behind and through the back.

OFFSIDES AT A KICK
All players on the kicker's team must remain behind the kicker while the kick is taking place. If the player is in front of the kicker while the kick is taking place, they must not move until a player that was behind the kick, is able to pass them and subsequently put them onsides.

If the player is in front of the kicker, and standing in the general vicinity of where the ball is going to land, they must make an effort to retreat ten meters away from the predicted landing spot.

ACCIDENTAL OFFSIDES
When an offside player cannot avoid being touched by the ball or by a teammate carrying it, the player is accidentally offsides. If the player's team gains no advantage from this, they play continues. If the player's team gains an advantage, a scrum is formed with the opposing team throwing in the ball.

OFFSIDE AFTER A KNOCK-ON
When a player knocks on and a teammate in front of that player plays the ball, they are offsides. If that same player who played the ball prevented an opponent from gaining an advantage, that player is liable to sanction..

OFFSIDE AT THE SCRUM
Defending team's backline must remain five meters behind the hindmost foot of the scrum until the ball is out. The defending team's loose forwards must remain bound to the scrum until the ball has left the scrumhalf's hands, as indicated by the referee. The scrumhalf must remain behind the ball at all times if following the ball at the scrum. If they are not following the ball, they are to immediately drop to the hindmost foot of the scrum and not leave further than one meter width from the scrum.

ADVANTAGE
Advantage is the period of time after an infringement in which the non-offending side have the opportunity to gain sufficient territory or tactical opportunity to negate the need to stop the game due to the infringement. Usually from a knock forward or turnover of possession. The referee is the sole judge of whether or not a team has gained an advantage. He will indicate to the players when the advantage period is over.

FOUL PLAY
Anything a player does within the playing enclosure that is against the letter and spirit of the laws of the game. It includes obstruction, unfair play, repeated infringements, dangerous play, and misconduct, which is prejudicial to the game. Foul play will almost always result in a penalty, and potentially a player being sent off the field. This is of course down to the referee's discretion.

TOUCH

The term "kicked directly into touch," means that the ball was kicked into touch without landing on the playing area and without touching a player or the referee. When this happens, the lineout is awarded to the opposing team from in the line of where the kick was taken.

When a player or team collects the ball and that team moves the ball back into their 22m and then kicks the ball directly into touch, a lineout is awarded to the opposing team from in line of where the kick was taken.

When a player collects the ball in their 22m and kicks it directly into touch, the line out is awarded to the opposing team in line with where the ball went out.

PENALTY KICK

When a player kicks to touch from a penalty anywhere in the playing area, the throw-in is taken where the ball went into touch and awarded to the team who kicked it into touch.

FREE KICK

Outside the kicker's 22m - no gain in ground if the player decides to kick it directly into touch.

Inside the kicker's 22m - the throw-in is where the ball went into touch, if the kicker decides to kick it directly into touch.

If on either a penalty, a free kick, kickoff, or kick in general play, and the ball goes over the dead ball line, a scrum is awarded from where the kick took place.

From a missed penalty goal, the ball goes over the dead ball line. The players restarted with a 22m dropout.

LINE-OUT

The purpose of the line-out is to restart play, quickly, safely and fairly, after the ball has got into touch, with a throw-in between two lines of players.

- The two lines of players set up between the 5-15m line.

- There must be a meter gap between the two lines.

- The minimum no. of players for a line-out to form is 2 players from each team.

- The team throwing the ball in the line-out decides on the maximum no. of players in the line-out.

- The opposing team may have fewer line-out players, but they must not have more.

- After the line-out has formed but, but before the ball has been thrown in, a player must not hold, push, charge into or obstruct an opponent.

- The ball must be thrown straight down the middle of the line-out.

- The two jumpers are not allowed to obstruct or pull down their opposition jump.

- The line-out ends/ball is out once the ball has left the jumpers hands.

SCRUM

The purpose of the scrum is to restart play quickly, safely and fairly, after a minor infringement or a stoppage.

- The scrum is formed in the field of play with eight players from each team, bound together in three rows.

- The scrum must remain stable, and players must maintain their weight - no twisting, dipping or collapsing or falling.

- A front row player must not lift or force a player up.

- A player may not use their hands to hook the ball back, only their feet.

- A player may not hold another opposition player in the scrum other than the props binding.

- The ball is out when the Eighthman's shoulders come off the scrum and they pick the ball up or when the ball leaves the scrumhalf's hands.

MARK

To make a mark, a player must be on or behind that players 22m line. The player must make a clean catch direct from an opponent's kick and at the same time shout, "MARK".

- A mark cannot be made from a kick-off or a restart kick.

- A free kick is awarded for a mark. The place for the kick is the place of the mark.

> I told the team to remember the three D's of rugby. Dackle, Dackle, Dackle.
>
> - Peter Fatialofa (joke made during a speech)

10. REFEREE SIGNALS

11. BASIC RUGBY GLOSSARY

A

ADVANTAGE - is the period of time after an infringement in which the non-offending side have the opportunity to gain sufficient territory or tactical opportunity to negate the need to stop the game due to the infringement. The referee will call the word, 'advantage' and indicate with his arm pointed 90 degrees in the direction to the non-offending team.

ANKLE TAP - When the tackler approaches from behind and taps or hooks the ball carriers foot causing him to stumble or fall.

ASSISTANT REFEREE - Also known as the touch judge or the linesman.

B

BINDING - Grasping firmly onto another player's body, usually between the shoulder and hips.

BLACK DOT - A mark in the center of the crossbar connecting the goal posts. Mostly used by commentators when suggesting the kick went straight through the middle of the posts.

BLITZ DEFENSE - a high-risk defensive system whereby defenders attempt to rush the attacking team by running up at speed to pressure the attackers.

BLOOD-BIN - When a player is escorted off the field of play to address an open wound and stop the flow of blood.

BOX-KICK - This is a kick taken by the scrumhalf from behind a scrum, maul or ruck where the player attempts to kick a contestable box into a clear box of space or clear the ball out of the field of play.

BREAKDOWN - This refers to a short period of time after a tackle has taken place where both teams compete for possession of the ball until the ball is effectively won and the next phase begins.

C

CHARGE-DOWN - When a defensive player blocks a kick with apart of his body. It is not considered a knock forward, and all offsides do not apply after the ball has left the players body.

COUNTER RUCKING - If a team (usually the team that took the ball into contact) has secured the ball at a ruck, and the other team is able to force them off the ball and secure possession themselves. The player/s counter rucking must come from an onside position, through the gate of the ruck and stay on feet at all times.

CHOKE TACKLE - A term used to describe a tackle in which the tackler attempts to keep the ball carrier on his feet to gain a turnover.

CROSS-FIELD KICK - An attacking kick which goes from one side of the field to the other. Often used nearer to the defending team'stry line.

D

DRIFT DEFENSE - A defensive strategy used by a team to force the opposition near to the touchline.

DEAD BALL - When the ball is out of play. This happens when the ball has gone outside of the playing area, or when the referee has blown the whistle to indicate a stoppage in play.

DUMMY RUNNER - When a player on the attacking team runs towards the opposition as if running onto a pass, only for the ball to be passed to another player.

DUMP TACKLE - A tackle technique whereby the tackler wraps his arms around the ball carrier, lifts him in the air, before driving him into the ground.

F

FOUL PLAY - Defined as the deliberate infringement of the laws of the game.

FREE KICK - Also called a short arm penalty. Usually awarded to a team for a technical offense committed. A free kick is signaled by the referee, with a bent arm raised in the air.

FRONT ROW - Refers to the front row of the scrum (loosehead prop, hooker, tighthead prop).

FULL HOUSE - Scoring a try, conversion, penalty, and drop goal in the same match.

G

GOAL LINE - Another term used for Try-line

GOAL POSTS - Another term used for the actual rugby posts stationed on both goal lines.

GOOSE-STEP - A sidestep made famous by Australian legend, David Campese whereby a player uses a specific running technique of slowing down, make a small hop in the air and then sprinting off upon landing and sometimes in a different direction. Its purpose is to stop the defender and confuse him into which direction the attacker will be going.

GRUBBER - Is a type of kick roll end over end along the ground produces irregular bounces making it difficult for the defender to pick the ball up.

H

HALFTIME - The interval between two halves, (10min long in 15's, 2min long in 7's).
HANDOFF - An action taken by the ball carrier to fend off an opponent by using the palm of their hand.
HALF-BACK - Another word used for a scrum-half.
HIGH TACKLE - An illegal tackle where the tackler grasps the ball carrier above the line of his/her shoulder.
HALF BREAK - When a player gets through the defensive line but is partially tackled, (not to ground).
HELD UP - When an attacking player is wrapped up by defenders and is unable to make their way to ground. A referee would inform the players that a maul is now formed. If the attacking team is unable to use the ball in a timely fashion, the referee will award a scrum to the defending team. A ball can also be 'held up' by a defending team while a ball carrier is attempting to ground the ball for a try.

I

INTERCEPTION - Gaining possession of the ball by catching a pass meant for an opponent.
IN GOAL AREA - As it often referred to in USA as the 'end zone'. In goal is the space between the try-line and the dead ball line.

K

KICK - is made by hitting the ball with your foot.

L

LIFTING - Self-explanatory term at the line-out or kick-off where the jumper is raised into the air.
LATCHER - The play who binds himself to the ball carrier in open play usually to drive him through the point of contact from behind.
LATE TACKLE - Is a tackle on a player who has already passed or kicked the ball away. It is illegal and is a penalizable offence.
LINE BREAK - An action where ball carrier gets through and behind the defensive line without being tackled.
LINE-SPEED - Used to refer to the speed at which the defensive line is coming up, putting pressure on the attacking side.

M

MARK - When a player executes a clean catch in their 22m, following a kick from an opposition player in general play. To call a 'mark', the player must shout 'MARK' as he or she catches it.

MAUL - 1). When a ball carrier is held up by the opposition. If the attacking team is unable to make use of the ball in a timely fashion, the referee will award a scrum to the defending team.

2). A line-out driving maul, basically 'legalized obstruction' is when an attacking team will bring the maul down at the line-out and create a protective mass of bodies while moving the ball to the back of the maul. The maul must move forward or else the ref will warn attacking team to 'use it or lose it' - if the maul becomes stationary and the attacking team is unable to play the ball then a scrum is awarded to the defending team.

MISMATCH - A one-on-one situation whereby attacking team has a massive advantage.

N

NOT STRAIGHT - A referee's call when the lineup throw or scrum feed is not put in incorrectly resulting in a turnover of possession.

O

OBSTRUCTION - An offence whereby a player deliberately impedes an opponent who does not have the ball.

OFFSIDE LINE - An imaginary line across the ground formed by a ruck, maul, scrum or kick. A player is offside when he/she is forward of the relevant offside line.

ONSIDE - A player is onside whenever he or she is behind the relevant offside line for the particular phase of play.

OFFLOAD - A short pass made by a player in contact or post contact off the ground in an attempt to avoid a breakdown and create continuity.

ON THE FULL - When a ball is kicked directly out of the field of play without bouncing inside the field of play first.

OPENSIDE - Refers to the broadside of the field in relation to the scrum or breakdown of play.

OVERLAP - A situation whereby there are more attacking players on one side of the field than that of defenders.

P

PACK - Another name used for forward players.
PASSING - Transferring the ball between teammates by throwing it.
PENALTY - Penalties are awarded for serious infringements like dangerous play, offside and handling the ball on the ground in a ruck. Penalties are signalled by the referee with a straight arm raised in the air.
PHASE - A phase is the period of time the ball is in play between breakdowns.
PLACE KICK - The kicking style commonly used when kicking for a penalty goal or a conversion. It involves placing the ball on the ground. To keep the ball in position, a plastic tee is sometimes used. Professional foul - a deliberate act of foul play.
POP PASS - A very short, sympathetic pass.
PUNT - A kick whereby the ball is dropped from the player's hand or hands and kicked before it touches the ground.

R

RED CARD - When a player is ordered off the field of play for a serious offence and may not return to the field of play for that match.
RUCK - A ruck is formed when the ball is on the ground and two opposing players meet over the ball. The offside line becomes the last foot of the last man on each side of the ruck and players compete for the ball by attempting to drive one another from the area and to 'ruck' the ball backward with their feet.

S

SCRUM - When 8 forwards from each bind together and pushing against each other while competing for the ball which is put in by the scrumhalf.
SET PIECE - A collective term for the scrum, line-out and sometimes the restart.

T

TAP KICK - A type of kick used by players on penalties or free kicks to restart the play. The player momentarily releases the ball from his hands and taps it with his foot or lower leg and then quickly catches it again.

TEST MATCH - A match between two international teams is called a Test Match.
TRY - Primary method of scoring, worth 5 points.
TUNNEL - The gap between the two front rows of the scrum or the space down the middle of the lineup between the two forward packs.

WHEELING - A scrum that has rotated between 90 degrees is referred to as 'wheeled'.

UNCONTESTED SCRUM - Is the same as a normal scrum, except the teams do not compete for the ball. The team throwing in the ball must win it, and neither team is allowed to push. This takes place when there are not enough specialized front row players available at a specific time.

YELLOW CARD - A card shown to a player who has been cautioned and temporarily suspended for ten minutes playing time.

12. ALTERNATIVE TERMS AND ANALOGIES

CODEHEAD - A term used to describe a player obsessed with the game. A studious rugby nerd.

MEAT PIE - Try.

WORM BURNER - Kick intended to go skyward but ends up skimming embarrassingly across the turf.

FALCON - When a ball connects with a player's head.

THE SHEDS - Changing or locker rooms.

RIDING THE PINE - Sitting on the bench.

ARGY BARGY - Pushing and shoving.

BOKING - Faking a lineout throw in, (illegal and leads to a free kick to the opposition).

BLOOD BIN - When a player is bleeding and led off the field to get treated.

UP THE GUTS - To play direct up the middle of the field into the opposition.

DUMMY - An attacking ruse when a player deceives an opponent by faking to pass it.

GARRYOWEN - An up and under kick, short in distance but great in height.

HAKA - A traditional Maori dance performed by New Zealand All Blacks before a test match.

THE PILL - The ball.

PILFER - To poach the ball away from the opposition at the breakdown.

BILL - William Webb Ellis trophy.

TRUCK AND TRAILER - An act of obstruction in a maul leading to a penalty.

CAULIFLOWER EAR - A deformity of the ear caused by attrition and rubbing of the head usually in the scrum.

HOSPITAL PASS - A pass received almost immediately before getting smashed in a tackle.

WHEELS/TOE - Term referred to running speed of a player.

IN THE FRIDGE - A term used to describe a player attempting to add on physical bulk.

JACKAL - Player is attempting to pilfer at the ruck.

SEED - Term generally used to describe a very good pass.

THE HONEY BADGER - Iconic former Wallaby winger, Nick Cummins.

PINNED HIS EARS BACK - To set off in hot pursuit of the try-line.

CRASHBALL - An attacking running line, flat and directly into a defensive wall.

KILLING THE BALL - When a defensive player purposefully lies over the ball in an attempt to prohibit the attack from playing it.

SNIPERED - When a player randomly loses footing/balance and falls, out of the picture of play.

DIRT TRACKERS - Term used to refer to non-playing squad/B-team.

To play rugby you need three things: a good pass, a good tackle and a good excuse."
- Anon

13. BANTER 101:

Some relevant and irrelevant content that may help you win an argument (or start one) and may even give you the decisive winning point in a pub quiz one day.

SIR RICHIE - Richard McCaw, the former All Blacks openside flanker and captain is the most capped player of all time with 149 Test matches. He has also captained the All Blacks to two World Cup titles and won World Player of the Year a record 3 times. He has seven Rugby Championship/Tri-Nations title and four Super Rugby titles. He also has a pilot's license. And they say nobody is perfect.

SUZIE - South Africa hosted the 1995 World Cup and claimed a memorable extra time 15-12 win over the All Blacks in the final with a legendary drop goal from Joel Stransky. However, many of the All Black players were allegedly ill on the day, with claims being made that their food was poisoned at their hotel on the day of the game. The woman who apparently did the deed was named Suzie. Wonder how she feels about Joel stealing her thunder?

THE ULTIMATE QUOTE - "We didn't have 60,000 South Africans, we had 43 million South Africans" - Springbok Captain Francois Pienaar's famous words when asked about winning the World Cup Final in front of a sold-out Ellis Park in Johannesburg in 1995.

ARE YOU NUTS? - Wayne 'Buck' Shelford, the legendary All Blacks flanker once had his scrotum ripped open by a stray stud from an opponent's boot in a Test match against France in 1986. That would be enough to make most folks retire and never look at a rugby ball again. Not Buck though. He had one of the trainers stitch it up so he could carry on playing.

KNIGHTS OF THE OVAL TABLE - To date, there have been 12 men that have received Knighthood from the Queen. They are in order: Wilson Whineray, Brian Lochore, Colin Meads, Clive Woodward, Ian McGeechan, Fred Allen, John Graham, Graham Henry, John Kirwan, Gordon Tietjens, Gareth Edwards and Michael Jones. Only Woodward (England), McGeechan (Scotland) and Edwards (Wales) are non-New Zealanders on the list.

FROM A SHIPLAKE RUGBY PARENT:

One of my friends asked "Why do you pay so much money and spend so much time running around for your son to play rugby?" Well I have a confession to make: I don't pay for my son's rugby training or his kit, mouthguard or boots. Or even his hundreds of rugby balls.
So, if I am not paying for rugby, what am I paying for?

- I pay for those moments when my boy becomes so tired he feels like quitting but doesn't..
- I pay for the opportunity that my boy can have and will have to make life-long friendships.
- I pay for the chance that he may have amazing coaches that will teach him that rugby is not just about game plans but about life.
- I pay for my child to learn to be disciplined.
- I pay for my boy to learn to take care of his body.
- I pay for my son to learn to work with others and to be a proud, supportive, kind and respectful team member.
- I pay for my child to learn to deal with disappointment, when he doesn't get that try he hoped for, or dropped the ball despite having practiced a thousand times, but still gets up and is determined to do his BEST next time...
- I pay for my boy to learn to make and accomplish goals.
- I pay for my son to learn that it takes hours and hours and hours and hours of hard work and practice to create a champion, and that success does not happen overnight.
- I pay so that my son can be on the pitch instead of in front of a screen...

I could go on but, to be short, I don't pay for rugby; I pay for the opportunities that rugby provides my child to develop attributes that will serve him well throughout his life, and give him the opportunity to bless the lives of others. From what I have seen for many years, I think it is a great investment!

10 THINGS COACHES LOVE IN A PLAYER:

1. MANNERS
2. HONESTY
3. RESPECT
4. CHARACTER
5. STRONG WORK ETHIC
6. FIGHTING SPIRIT / GRIT
7. ACCOUNTABILITY
8. COACHABLE
9. HUMBLE
10. POSITIVE BODY LANGUAGE

CHARLIE PURDON

Charlie was born and raised in, 'rugby mad' South Africa and fell in love with the game when he began attending boarding school at a young age. Post schooling he has been fortunate to travel and partly make a career in rugby as a player, most recently in Southern California, USA. Charlie is passionate about the sport and considers himself a student of the game. He is currently the Director and Head Coach of a high performance Rugby Academy in San Diego, focusing on fundamental skill development. He also plays his own rugby for Old Mission Beach Athletic Club in the Pacific Rugby Premiership.

WARWICK AUSTIN

Warwick is a walking sports encyclopedia and the self proclaimed 'Bantersaurus Rex'. Like most South Africans, rugby pumps through his veins.

A journalist by trade, Warwick graduated from Rhodes University and has worked as a presenter and commentator on SuperSport, one of the biggest sports broadcasters in the world.

Apart from writing for various print and online publications in South Africa, he has also branched out into the realm of marketing. This has seen him work on the conceptual and creative elements of advertising campaigns around the FIFA World Cup and Super Rugby - of which some of the work has global award nominations.

Still actively involved as a player, he plays for the second oldest club in South Africa, Wanderers Rugby Football Club in Johannesburg, where his keen sense of self preservation coupled with a nose for the tryline ensures that his laundry bill stays low.

He also met Pele once and now counts him among his closest friends.

Made in the USA
Middletown, DE
14 February 2023